The Magic of Peanut Butter

The Magic of
Peanut Butter

100 New & Favorite Recipes by Skippy®

Sterling Publishing Co., Inc. New York
A Sterling/Chapelle Book

Chapelle, Ltd., Inc., P.O. Box 9252, Ogden, UT 84409

(801) 621-2777 • (801) 621-2788 Fax

e-mail: chapelle@chapelleltd.com

Web site: www.chapelleltd.com

Library of Congress Cataloging-in-Publication Data available

The magic of peanut butter : 100 new & favorite recipes / by Skippy.
 p. cm.
 "A Sterling/Chapelle book."
 Includes index.
 ISBN 1-4027-1601-X
 1.   Cookery (Peanut butter)

TX814.5.P38M43 2005
641.6'56596--dc22

                                                    2005012843

10 9 8 7 6 5 4 3 2

Published by Sterling Publishing Co., Inc.

387 Park Avenue South, New York, NY 10016

©2005 by Unilever

Distributed in Canada by Sterling Publishing

c/o Canadian Manda Group, 165 Dufferin Street

Toronto, Ontario, Canada M6K 3H6

Distributed in Australia by Capricorn Link (Australia) Pty. Ltd.

P. O. Box 704, Windsor, NSW 2756, Australia

Printed and Bound in China

All Rights Reserved

Sterling ISBN 1-4027-1601-X

For information about custom editions, special sales, premium and
corporate purchases, please contact Sterling Special Sales Department at
800-805-5489 or specialsales@sterlingpub.com.

Contents

History of Skippy®

CHAPTER ONE

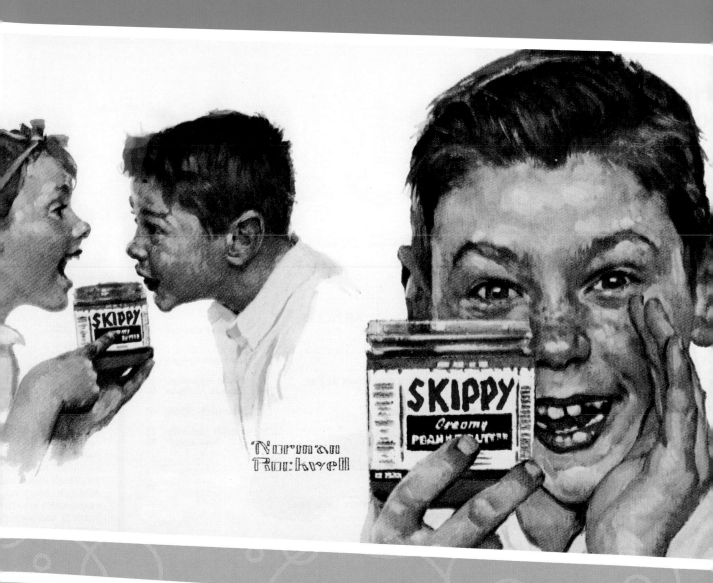

Introduction

For most of us, the peanut butter sandwich was a fundamental part of our childhood experience. Peanut butter, after all, is the number-one consumed food among kids. But peanut butter has a lot more to contribute to our diets than peanut butter sandwiches. After all, it's a food that belongs to the fruits and vegetables group but its reputation as a great source of protein leads many to mistaken it for a part of the meat group. It is, perhaps, one of the most flexible and nutritious foods to ever hit the market.

In this cookbook, you'll find tasty, satisfying recipes for morning, noon and night. Start the day with the protein-packed Banana Breakfast Drink or send the kids off to school with crunchy Banana Breakfast Nuggets. Impress dinner guests with Creamy Peanut-Garlic Dressing on salad, followed by Peanut & Lime Shrimp Sauté. Celebrate the New Year with international treats such as Peanut Coconut Thai Soup and Chicken Sate with Peanut Sauce. We have gathered over one hundred recipes from the United States and around the globe that will delight and nourish the whole family.

The Early Days of Peanut Butter

So how did the peanut butter phenomenon come about? The unknown physician who, in the late nineteenth century, asked a foods manufacturer to market peanut paste as a protein substitute for those who couldn't chew meat would attribute its popularity to the protein. So would John Harvey Kellogg, who, five years later, first introduced peanut butter as we know it; he, too, was in search of a nutritious protein substitute for patients.

But today people champion the peanut not only as a high-protein food, but also as a high-fiber legume. As the public becomes increasingly weight-conscious, dieters sing the praises of this hearty, fulfilling food because while it is rich in nutrients, it contains almost no trans fat, or saturated fat.

A PAID TESTIMONIAL FROM **BERT LAHR** FOR SKIPPY PEANUT BUTTER

if you like peanuts, you'll like Skippy

But there's more to the peanut butter story—read on to learn just why America and later the world would come to love and rely on peanut butter.

The History of the Peanut

Goobers, monkey nuts, ground peas, guinea seeds—all names of the ever popular peanut. But where did the peanut come from? Archeologists speculate that the peanut originated in Brazil or Peru when they found peanut-shaped jars decorated with images of peanuts. Jars full of peanuts have been found in ancient Incan graves.

Missionaries and traders carried peanuts to Spain, Africa, and the New World, where they were planted throughout the South in the United States. Peanuts grew in popularity there with the Civil War, when Union and Confederate soldiers alike drew nourishment from them when food supplies were low. But the peanut's heyday would come in 1870, when P. T. Barnum's circus sold hot roasted peanuts to crowds across the country. Soon they were sold at ballparks and movie theaters as a novel, delicious treat.

By 1903, George Washington Carver found over three hundred practical applications for the peanut—in products as far-ranging as soap, mayonnaise, dairy products, medicine, ink, bleach, and axle grease, just to name a few. For a long time, some believed that Carver invented peanut butter. However, the history of peanut butter reaches farther back in time—back to the beginning of the Gilded Age, a decade before the turn of the century.

The Peanut Butter Timeline

1890 Ground peanut paste emerges as a high-protein supplement when an unknown physician asks George A. Bayle to produce it for people who can't chew meat.

1895 Peanut butter is born. John Harvey Kellogg provides patients in a sanitarium he and his brother own with peanut butter made of steamed peanuts.

1896 Joseph Lambert develops and markets a hand-operated peanut grinder—a predecessor to the mechanized peanut grinders used today.

1904 C. H. Sumner introduces peanut butter at the St. Louis Universal Exposition. The debut is phenomenal, boosting peanut butter's popularity around the globe.

1914 Several dozen commercial brands of peanut butter appear on the market.

1923 Joseph Rosefield develops a process for producing peanut butter that prevents oil separation from the peanut butter, which increases its shelf life to up to a year.

1929 Black Tuesday initiates the Great Depression. The government restricts supply to help peanut farmers endure the financial disaster.

1933 Rosefield Packing Company registers Skippy® as a trademark for peanut butter. Soon after, Rosefield introduces chunky peanut butter, mixing chopped peanuts in with the regular recipe. Other peanut butter producers follow his lead.

1935 Skippy® introduces peanut butter in a wide-mouth jar.

1940 Production of Skippy® Peanut Butter begins at a new plant in Minneapolis, Minnesota.

1941 The U.S. enters World War II. Peanut butter is considered a cheap alternative to meat and butter amid commodity controls. Peanut butter and jelly sandwiches become an important part of military rations.

1944 Rosefield Packing Company completes an eleven-year effort to register the Skippy® trademark in all forty-eight states and Hawaii.

1945 Rosefield opens a Skippy® Peanut Butter plant in Portsmouth, Virginia.

1946 Rosefield Packing Company is issued a patent for making peanut butter. Two years later, Rosefield obtains a federal U.S. trademark for Skippy® Peanut Butter.

1955 Best Foods, Inc., which will become Bestfoods, purchases the Rosefield Packing Company and its flagship brand, Skippy®, committing to broaden and improve their offerings.

1956 Production of Skippy® Peanut Butter begins at the Bestfoods plant in Dallas, Texas.

1963 Norman Rockwell creates illustrations to promote Skippy® Peanut Butter.

1973 Bestfoods introduces Skippy® Super Chunk® Peanut Butter.

1977 Production of Skippy® Peanut Butter begins at a new plant in Little Rock, Arkansas.

1994 Bestfoods introduces Skippy® Reduced Fat Creamy® Peanut Butter spread to satisfy an increasingly health-conscious public.

1996 Skippy® launches a more "peanutty" flavored peanut butter.

1998 Skippy® launches an easier-to-spread reduced-fat peanut butter spread.

2000 Unilever acquires Bestfoods and with it, the Skippy® brand. Studies reveal a number of nutritional benefits associated with midfat diets that include peanut butter.

2003 In a continuing effort to offer consumers variety, the company introduces Skippy® Squeeze Stix as a nutritious, convenient snack for increasingly busy families.

2004 Skippy® Snack Bars emerge as hearty, convenient snacks. The snack bars feature layers of peanut butter and granola, along with other popular ingredients. Carb Options™ Creamy Peanut Spread is introduced for use as part of a low-carb diet. This creamy spread has three grams net carbs per serving.[1]

2005 Skippy® Trail Mix Bars are introduced, which combine peanut butter, peanuts, wholesome granola and other ingredients. Skippy® Natural Peanut Butter Spread also appears on store shelves. Unlike some natural peanut butters, this doesn't need to be stirred before using.

[1] See Skippy® as a Nutritious Choice pages 14–15

History of Skippy®

Skippy® Today

The ability of Skippy® products to satisfy America's appetite for variety and flavor remains part of the reason the U.S. is the world's largest peanut butter producer and consumer today. Skippy® has emerged as an innovator in the peanut butter category, by producing convenient peanut butter snacks such as Skippy® Squeeze Stix, Skippy® Squeez' It, Skippy® Snack Bars, and Skippy® Trail Mix Bars. In addition, Skippy® products also include better-for-you choices, such as Carb Options™ Creamy Peanut Spread and Skippy® Natural Peanut Butter Spread. As ongoing research reveals the proven nutritional benefits of peanut butter as a high-fiber, high-protein, nutrient-rich member of the fruits-and-vegetables food group, its popularity among adults and children alike continues to grow.

Skippy® as a Nutritious Choice

• Peanut butter contains most of the twenty-two amino acids (protein) the body needs for healthy muscles, bones, blood, and body organs. Combine it with whole-grain bread in a peanut butter sandwich to get a full range of amino acids.[1]

• Though peanuts are known foremost as an excellent source of protein, few realize they are actually part of the fruits-and-vegetables food group. The USDA recommends eating at least five to thirteen servings from this group per day. Peanuts are high-fiber, high-protein legumes—a great way to help fulfill part of daily vegetable requirements while satisfying your appetite and energizing your body with protein.[2]

[1] http://kidshealth.org/kid/stay_healthy/food/protein.html
[2] http://news.findlaw.com/prnewswire/20050112/12jan2005184412.html; see also, http://www.jaen.org/cgi/content/full/20/1/5

- Like enriched bread and grains, citrus fruits, and dark leafy vegetables, peanuts are a good source of the B vitamin folic acid. Folic acid helps reduce the risk of some birth defects among pregnant women.

- Peanut butter has a low Glycemic Index, which makes it a smart choice for people with diabetes. Also, peanuts have magnesium, which can help prevent Type 2 diabetes.[3]

- A Harvard School of Public Health nurses' health study revealed that women who consumed more nuts and peanuts tended to weigh less. At the same time, a USDA survey of over 10,000 Americans showed that peanut and peanut butter eaters tended to have lower body mass indexes (BMI), a measure of body fat based on height and weight.[4]

- All Skippy® Peanut Butter and peanut butter spreads are gluten-free. Some people are highly sensitive to gluten, a collection of proteins that can cause stomach pain and other problems in individuals with Celiac disease.[5]

- One hundred ninety calories—found in one 2-tablespoon serving of peanut butter—can go a long way in fending off hunger while providing the body with protein, vitamins, and fiber.

  - Carb Option™ Creamy Peanut Spread counts as only 3 grams. From five total carbohydrates, subtract two grams of fiber, as this has minimal impact on blood sugar.

[3] see note [2]
[4] see note [2]
[5] http://www.nutramed.com/celiac/celiacintro.htm

People Love Peanut Butter

Why is peanut butter so popular? Well, aside from the fact that the nutrition in peanuts speaks for itself, people obviously think that it tastes great! Consider some of the statistics listed here;

- Annual consumption of peanut butter is around eight hundred million pounds—that's enough peanut butter to form a line of eighteen-ounce jars stretching almost one and one-third time around the world.

- Nobody consumes as much peanut butter as Americans; however, it is popular in Canada, Holland, England, Germany, and Saudi Arabia, and it's gaining popularity throughout Eastern Europe.

- The average American child will eat fifteen hundred peanut butter sandwiches by the time he or she graduates from high school.

- In the last year, more than 75% of all American families purchased peanut butter.

- Americans eat about three pounds of peanut butter per person each year, totaling about five hundred million pounds for the country's population—enough to cover the floor of the Grand Canyon.

- Americans eat enough peanut butter in a year to make over ten billion peanut butter and jelly sandwiches (with an estimated two tablespoons of peanut butter per sandwich).

Are you a Top Grade nut nut?

Are you the kind of nut who's nuts about the taste of top rank, top notch, top grade nuts?
Then stand easy and hear this:
A truly top nut is the U.S. Grade No. 1 peanut. (Saluted everywhere as the "nut nut's nut.")
Only two things give you the fine, fresh-roasted flavor of fancy U.S. Grade No. 1 peanuts. Peanuts themselves and Skippy Peanut Butter. Skippy® is peanuts—No. 1 Peanuts in their most spreadable, edible form.
And because of the secret patented way it's made, only Skippy captures and keeps that elusive, fresh-roasted flavor for you—right down to the last delicious dab.
So, whether you rank as a nut nut or not, the fact is **if you like peanuts—you'll like Skippy.** America's top-selling peanut butter.

Fun Facts for Kids

Peanut butter is for kids, right? Few kids have gone through life without peanut butter. But here's a little-known secret: Grown-ups eat more peanut butter than kids do! In fact, there's a group out there that calls itself the Adult Peanut Butter Lovers' Fan Club. This club includes celebrities like President Bill Clinton, Cher, Madonna, Billy Joel, Julia Roberts, Bill Cosby, and Michael J. Fox, and more!

And there's a lot more you might not know about peanut butter. Here are more fun facts you can share with your friends.

What are peanuts?

Peanuts aren't nuts! They are actually legumes, like peas, lentils, and beans, and they grow in pods under the ground. Nuts like almonds and walnuts grow on trees.

How do peanuts become peanut butter?

Peanut farmers (called growers) harvest peanuts in the fall then sell them to peanut shellers. The shellers use special machines to remove the peanut kernels from the shells. After the peanuts are cleaned and sorted by size, the shellers ship them by train to peanut butter makers like Skippy®. The peanuts are then ground and processed into peanut butter.

When peanut butter was first created, producers found that the peanut oil separated from the peanut butter. But in 1922, the creator of Skippy®, Joseph Rosefield, developed a process to blend the butter in a way that prevented oil separation, which explains why the Skippy® Peanut Butter we eat today is creamy and easy to spread.

How much peanut butter does it take to cover the floor of the Grand Canyon?

The same amount of peanut butter that all Americans combined eat each year: five hundred million pounds. The average American eats three pounds of peanut butter a year! America is populated by nearly three hundred million people, and three out of four households regularly eat peanut butter. If the average American is eating three pounds of peanut butter . . . well, let's just say this—that's a lot of peanut butter!

How big was the world's largest peanut butter and jelly sandwich?

Forty feet long: that's about ten seven-year-old children lined up head-to-toe. The sandwich was made with 150 pounds of peanut butter and 50 pounds of jelly. It was created on November 6, 1993 in Peanut, Pennsylvania.

Which U.S. presidents were once peanut farmers?

Your friends might know President Jimmy Carter was a peanut farmer. But do they know President Thomas Jefferson was a peanut farmer, too? By the way, baseball Hall of Famer Catfish Hunter is another well-known peanut farmer.

What is arachibutyrophobia?

Have you ever tried to sing the ABCs with a mouthful of peanut butter? Not pretty. Arachibutyrophobes don't think so either. Arachibutyrophobia (pronounced I-RA-KID-BU-TI-RO-PHO-BI-A) is the fear of peanut butter getting stuck to the roof of your mouth.

Are you a nut nut?

A nut nut is a person who is nuts about the fun of eating nuts.
A prime favorite of the true nut nut is the fresh-roasted U.S. Grade No. 1 peanut. Truly a nut nut's nut.
In all the world, only two things taste exactly like fancy, fresh-roasted No. 1 peanuts.

Peanuts themselves and Skippy Peanut Butter. You see, Skippy is peanuts—peanuts in their most spreadable, edible form. And it's made in a secret, patented way that keeps every peerless, priceless particle of that true, exact, fresh-

roasted peanut taste. None of it gets away. So, if you're a nut nut—in other words, **if you like peanuts— you'll like Skippy.** Skippy Peanut Butter. (The one nut nuts are nuts about.)

Who prefers chunky-style peanut butter and who prefers creamy style?

Six out of ten peanut butter lovers prefer chunky-style peanut butter over creamy style. Folks on the East Coast prefer creamy style peanut butter, which means many of our fans can be found on the West Coast, where consumers most often opt for chunky-style peanut butter. And another thing—men seem to prefer chunky style peanut butter while women and children prefer creamy style. Which is your favorite?

What came first, peanut butter or jelly?

The jelly. Although peanut butter was invented in 1895, it didn't hit store shelves until 1914. Meanwhile, jelly had a running start. Jams and jellies had been made for centuries—first in Middle Eastern countries, then in Europe. Although jelly was sold long before peanut butter, 96% of people spread the peanut butter on the bread before the jelly.

How many peanuts does it take to make a jar of peanut butter?

It takes almost 850 peanuts to make an eighteen-ounce jar of Skippy® Peanut Butter!

Capture America's most wanted nut!

Don't let the flimsy disguise fool you. America's most wanted nut is a U.S. No.1 peanut. Nut nuts (persons who are nuts about the fun of eating nuts) all over America are nuts about this nut. It is truly a nut's nut. Yet capturing its fine, fresh-roasted flavor is a breeze.

Simply pick up a jar of Skippy® In all the world, only two things taste exactly like fancy, fresh-roasted No. 1 peanuts. Peanuts themselves and Skippy Peanut Butter. Because of the exclusive, patented way it's made, Skippy arrests, detains and

keeps that fresh-roasted, U.S. Grade No. 1 flavor for you from first dip to last dab. So reward yourself! Nut nut or not, **if you like peanuts — you'll like Skippy.** America's largest selling, most wanted peanut butter.

Breakfast Breakouts

CHAPTER TWO

Banana & Peanut Butter Muffins

12 muffins Prep Time: 15 minutes Cook Time: 20 minutes

2⅓ cups all-purpose flour

1½ tsp. baking powder

1 tsp. baking soda

⅓ cup margarine

¼ cup Skippy® Creamy Peanut Butter

½ cup sugar

2 eggs

1 cup milk

2 ripe bananas, mashed

1. Preheat oven to 400°F. Grease 12-cup muffin pan or line with paper cup cake liners; set aside.
2. In medium bowl, combine flour, baking powder and baking soda; set aside.
3. In large bowl, with electric mixer, beat margarine and Skippy® Creamy Peanut Butter until smooth. Add sugar and mix until light and fluffy, about 3 minutes. Beat in eggs. With mixer on low, alternately beat in flour mixture and milk combined with bananas until blended. Evenly spoon batter into prepared pan.
4. Bake 20 minutes or until toothpick inserted in centers comes out clean. On wire rack, cool 10 minutes; remove from pan and cool completely.

No Skippin' Breakfast Muffins

4 muffins Prep Time: 5 minutes

4 Tbsp. Skippy® Peanut Butter

2 English muffins, split and toasted

1 medium apple, cored and thinly sliced

1 banana, sliced

1. Spread 1 tablespoon Skippy® Peanut Butter on each muffin half. Top with sliced apple and banana.

Tip To make an even more wholesome snack, use whole wheat English muffins.

Peanut Butter Breakfast Muffins

12 muffins **Prep Time:** *15 minutes* **Cook Time:** *20 minutes*

1 cup oat flakes or bran flakes cereal with raisins, crushed

1½ cup all-purpose flour

½ cup sugar

1 Tbsp. baking powder

½ tsp. ground cinnamon

¼ tsp. salt

½ cup dried cherries or apricots

1¼ cups milk

¾ cup Skippy® Creamy Peanut Butter

1 egg

1 tsp. vanilla extract

1. Preheat oven to 400°F. Grease 12-cup muffin pan or line with paper cup cake liners; set aside.

2. In medium bowl, combine cereal, flour, sugar, baking power, cinnamon and salt. Stir in apricots; set aside.

3. In large bowl, with electric mixer, beat milk, Skippy® Creamy Peanut Butter, egg and vanilla until smooth. With mixer on low, add dry ingredients just until combined. Evenly spoon batter into prepared pan.

4. Bake 20 minutes or until toothpick inserted in centers comes out clean. On wire rack, cool 10 minutes; remove from pan and cool completely.

Breakfast Breakouts

Nutty Breakfast Rolls

4 servings **Prep Time:** *15 minutes*

½ cup Skippy® Peanut Butter

8 hot cooked pancakes

2 medium bananas, halved lengthwise, then crosswise

Maple syrup (optional)

1. Evenly spread Skippy® Peanut Butter on hot pancakes, then top with bananas; roll up.

2. Serve, if desired, cut in pieces with maple syrup.

Variation

Apple Cinnamon: Stir ¼ cup applesauce and ½ teaspoon ground cinnamon into Peanut Butter.

Cinnamon: Stir ½ teaspoon ground cinnamon into Peanut Butter.

Chocolate Chip: Stir ¼ cup semi-sweet chocolate chips into Peanut Butter.

Cinnamon Raisin: Stir ½ teaspoon ground cinnamon and ¼ cup raisins into Peanut Butter.

PB&J Oatmeal

1 serving **Prep Time:** *5 minutes*

1 Tbsp. Skippy® Peanut Butter

1 Tbsp. grape, strawberry, or raspberry jelly

1 cup your favorite hot cooked oatmeal

1. Stir Skippy® Peanut Butter and jelly into hot oatmeal.

Serving Suggestion

Top, if desired, with raisins or sliced fresh fruit.

Nutty Breakfast Rolls

Peanut Butter Scones with Grape Drizzle

8 scones Prep Time: *10 minutes* Cook Time: *18 minutes*

¼ cup Skippy® Creamy Peanut Butter

1 egg, slightly beaten

¾ cup milk

1 tsp. vanilla extract

2 cups all-purpose flour

¼ cup sugar

2½ tsp. baking powder

½ tsp. salt

¼ cup margarine

*Grape drizzle

1. Preheat oven to 400°F.

2. In medium bowl, with wire whisk, combine Skippy® Creamy Peanut Butter and egg until blended, then add milk and vanilla; set aside.

3. In large bowl, combine flour, sugar, baking powder and salt. With pastry blender or 2 knives, cut in margarine. Add peanut butter mixture and stir until dough forms.

4. On lightly floured surface, lightly knead dough with floured hands and shape into 9-inch circle. With floured knife, cut dough in half crosswise, then cut each half into 4 or 5 wedges. On cookie sheet, arrange wedges.

5. Bake 18 minutes or until golden. On wire rack, cool 2 minutes. Top scones with Grape Drizzle and serve warm.

Grape Drizzle: In small microwave-safe bowl, microwave ¼ cup grape jelly at HIGH 30 seconds or until melted, then add 1 cup confectioners sugar until combined.

Banana Breakfast Nuggets

4 servings **Prep Time:** *5 minutes* **Cook Time:** *30 seconds*

½ cup Skippy® Peanut Butter

2 bananas, cut into 2-inch pieces

1 cup your favorite breakfast cereal

1. In small microwave-safe bowl, microwave Skippy®
Peanut Butter at HIGH 30 seconds or until melted.

2. Dip bananas into Peanut Butter, then roll in cereal.
Chill until ready to serve.

Breakfast Breakouts

Toasted Monkey Sandwiches

2 servings **Prep Time:** *5 minutes* **Cook Time:** *4 minutes*

¼ cup Skippy® Peanut Butter

4 slices white, wheat or cinnamon-raisin bread

1 medium banana, sliced

1. Evenly spread Skippy® Peanut Butter on 2 bread slices, then top with banana and remaining bread slices.

2. In 12-inch nonstick skillet sprayed with nonstick cooking spray, cook sandwiches over medium heat until golden brown, about 4 minutes, turning once.

Skippy® Jammin' French Toast

4 servings **Prep Time:** *5 minutes* **Cook Time:** *5 minutes*

½ cup Skippy® Peanut Butter

8 slices white or whole wheat bread

½ cup grape, strawberry, or raspberry jelly

2 eggs

½ cup milk

1 Tbsp. margarine

1. Evenly spread Skippy® Peanut Butter on one side of 4 bread slices, then spread jelly on remaining bread slices. Assemble sandwiches.

2. In shallow dish, combine eggs and milk; beat thoroughly. Lightly dip sandwiches into egg mixture.

3. In 12-inch nonstick skillet, melt margarine over medium heat and lightly brown sandwiches, turning once.

Toasted Monkey Sandwiches

Peanutty Stuffed French Toast

4 servings **Prep Time: *5 minutes*** **Cook Time: *5 minutes***

½ cup Skippy® Peanut Butter

8 slices white or whole wheat bread

2 medium bananas, mashed

2 eggs

½ cup milk

1 Tbsp. margarine

1. Evenly spread Skippy® Peanut Butter on one side of 4 bread slices, then spread banana on remaining bread slices. Assemble sandwiches.
2. In shallow dish, combine eggs and milk; beat thoroughly. Lightly dip sandwiches into egg mixture.
3. In 12-inch nonstick skillet, melt margarine over medium heat and lightly brown sandwiches, turning once.

Bubblin' Nut & Fruitwich

4 servings **Prep Time:** *5 minutes* **Cook Time:** *1 minute*

¾ cup Skippy® Peanut Butter

4 English muffins, split and toasted

½ cup raisins

2 medium apples, cored and thinly sliced

8 tsp. firmly packed brown sugar

1. Spread Skippy® Peanut Butter on each muffin half. Top with raisins and apple slices, then sprinkle with brown sugar.
2. Broil 1 minute or until bubbling.

Variation For a Bubblin' Apple & Banana Fruitwich, add 3 to 4 banana slices to each muffin half before sprinkling with brown sugar.

Peanut Butter Banana Roll-ups

4 servings **Prep Time:** *5 minutes*

4 slices your favorite bread, crusts removed and flattened if desired

4 Tbsp. Skippy® Peanut Butter

2 medium bananas, cut in half crosswise

1. Spread each bread slice with 1 tablespoon Skippy® Peanut Butter.
2. Top with banana half and roll up. Slice, if desired, into ½-inch rounds.

Tip To make an even more wholesome snack, use whole wheat bread.

31

Skippy® Peanut Butter Breakfast Latte

2 servings **Prep Time: *5 minutes***

1 cup cold milk or vanilla soy milk

½ cup chilled brewed coffee

¼ cup Skippy® Creamy Peanut Butter

2 Tbsp. sugar

½ tsp. unsweetened cocoa powder

1. In blender, combine all ingredients. Blend until smooth. Serve immediately.

Breakfast Breakouts

1 container (6 oz.) vanilla or plain yogurt

½ cup 2% milk

¼ cup Skippy® Peanut Butter

1 medium banana, sliced

½ cup ice cubes (3 to 4)

1. In blender, process all ingredients except ice cubes.

2. Add ice cubes, one at a time, and process until blended.
Serve immediately.

The Lunch Box

CHAPTER THREE

On-the-Go Apple 'n Peanut Butter

1 serving **Prep Time: *5 minutes***

1 Granny Smith or other tart apple
1 Tbsp. Skippy® Peanut Butter

1. Evenly slice apple into 8 slices. Cut core and seeds from each slice.
2. Spread Skippy® Peanut Butter on both sides of each slice, then "glue" apple back together.
3. Tightly wrap in plastic wrap.

Tip These are great for kid's lunchboxes.

Elephant Tusk Wrap

2 Tbsp. Skippy® Peanut Butter

2 Tbsp. your favorite jelly

1 (8-in.) flour tortilla

1 small banana

1. Evenly spread Skippy® Peanut Butter then jelly on tortilla. Top with banana, then roll up.

Peanut Butter BLT Wraps

4 servings Prep Time: *5 minutes*

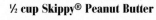

½ cup Skippy® Peanut Butter

4 (8-in.) flour tortillas

8 slices bacon, crisp-cooked

4 lettuce leaves

1 large tomato, sliced

1. Evenly spread Skippy® Peanut Butter on tortillas. Top with remaining ingredients; roll up.

2. To serve, cut each wrap in half.

Peanut Butter Banana Boats

2 servings **Prep Time: 5 minutes**

¼ cup Skippy® Peanut Butter

1 Tbsp. honey (optional)

½ tsp. ground cinnamon (optional)

2 hot dog buns, toasted if desired

1 medium banana, halved lengthwise or sliced

1. In small bowl, blend Skippy® Peanut Butter, honey and cinnamon.
2. Evenly spread peanut butter mixture in hot dog buns, then top with banana.

Tip To make an even more wholesome snack, use whole wheat bread in place of hot dog buns.

Peanut Butter & Fruit Rolls

1 serving Prep Time: *10 minutes*

1 slice whole wheat bread, crust removed

1 Tbsp. Skippy® Peanut Butter

1½ tsp. fruit spread or preserves

2 tsp. flaked coconut or crushed peanuts

1. With rolling pin or glass, completely flatten bread. Evenly spread Skippy® Peanut Butter and 1 teaspoon fruit spread on flattened bread, then roll up to make a pinwheel.

2. Spread remaining ½ teaspoon fruit spread on outside of pinwheel, then dip in coconut. Cut into bite-sized pieces.

Peanut Butter & Honey Sushi

1 serving Prep Time: *10 minutes*

1 slice whole wheat bread, crust removed

1 Tbsp. Skippy® Peanut Butter

1 tsp. honey

2 tsp. flaked coconut

1. With rolling pin or glass, completely flatten bread. Evenly spread Skippy® Peanut Butter on flattened bread, then roll up to make a pinwheel.

2. Spread honey on outside of pinwheel, then dip in coconut.

3. Cut into bite-sized pieces.

Peanut Butter & Fruit Rolls

Peanut Butter Roll-ups

1 serving **Prep Time: *5 minutes***

2 Tbsp. Skippy® Peanut Butter

1 (10-in.) whole wheat flour tortilla, warmed if desired

¼ cup Granny Smith apple, thinly sliced

1 Tbsp. raisins

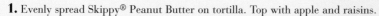

1. Evenly spread Skippy® Peanut Butter on tortilla. Top with apple and raisins.

2. Roll up and seal with Peanut Butter.

Chewy Trail Mix Peanut Butter Bars

36 bars Prep Time: 15 minutes Cook Time: 10 minutes

2½ cups crisp rice cereal

1¼ cups old fashioned cooking oats

1 cup chopped mixed dried fruit (raisins, apricots, cranberries, dates or apples)

1 cup chopped peanuts

¾ cup Skippy® Peanut Butter

¾ cup firmly packed brown sugar

¾ cup light corn syrup

½ cup unsweetened cocoa powder

1. In large bowl, combine cereal, oats, dried fruit and peanuts; set aside.
2. In small saucepan, combine Skippy® Peanut Butter, brown sugar and corn syrup and cook, stirring frequently, over medium heat until smooth; stir in cocoa powder. Pour peanut butter mixture over dry ingredients and mix well.
3. In foil-lined 13x9-inch baking pan, evenly press cereal mixture. Cool until set, then cut in bars.

The Lunch Box

PB&J Pita

1 serving **Prep Time: *5 minutes***

3 Tbsp. Skippy® Peanut Butter

3 Tbsp. grape, strawberry or raspberry jelly

1 medium-size pita bread, toasted if desired

1. Evenly spread Skippy® Peanut Butter and jelly on pita bread.

Serving Suggestion Top, if desired, with raisins, chopped apple or sliced banana.

2 servings Prep Time: *10 minutes* Cook Time: *5 minutes*

¼ cup Skippy® Peanut Butter

2 (10-in.) flour tortillas

1 medium banana, sliced

3 Tbsp. mini semi-sweet chocolate chips or ¼ cup mini marshmallows

1. Evenly spread Skippy® Peanut Butter on ½ of each tortilla. Top with banana, then chocolate.

2. Fold tortillas in half to form quesadillas.

3. In 12-inch nonstick skillet, cook quesadillas over medium-high heat, turning once, 5 minutes or until golden brown and chocolate is melted.

Microwave Directions: On microwave-safe dish, microwave prepared quesadillas at HIGH 45 seconds or until chocolate is melted.

Big E. Quesadillas

2 servings Prep Time: *10 minutes* Cook Time: *5 minutes*

¼ cup Skippy® Peanut Butter

2 (10-in.) flour tortillas

¼ cup of your favorite jelly or jam

1 medium banana, sliced

1. Evenly spread Skippy® Peanut Butter on ½ of each tortilla. Top with jelly, then bananas.

2. Fold tortillas in half to form quesadillas.

3. In 12-inch nonstick skillet, cook quesadillas over medium-high heat, turning once, 5 minutes or until golden brown.

Microwave Directions: On microwave-safe dish, microwave prepared quesadillas at HIGH 45 seconds or until heated through.

P. Nutty & Big E. Quesadillas

Snack Time

CHAPTER FOUR

Banana Surprise

1 serving **Prep Time: *5 minutes***

1 banana, halved lengthwise
1 Tbsp. Skippy® Peanut Butter
1 tsp. raisins

1. With teaspoon, slightly hollow the inside of one banana half.
2. Evenly spread Skippy® Peanut Butter down the center. Sprinkle with raisins, then top with remaining banana half.
3. Microwave at HIGH 15 seconds or until slightly warm.

Crispy Apple Wedges

1 serving **Prep Time: 5 minutes**

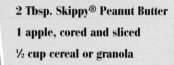

2 Tbsp. Skippy® Peanut Butter
1 apple, cored and sliced
½ cup cereal or granola

1. Spread Skippy® Peanut Butter on apple slices, then press in cereal.

Tip To make an even more wholesome snack, use unsweetened cereal or granola.

Peanut Butter 'N Yogurt Dip

about 1 cup dip **Prep Time: 5 minutes**

½ cup Skippy® Peanut Butter

1 container (8 oz.) vanilla or fruit flavored yogurt

1. In small bowl, blend Skippy® Peanut Butter with yogurt.

Serving Suggestion Serve, if desired, with sliced apples, carrots, cucumbers, bananas, or strawberries. Or . . . try as a breakfast spread on toasted bagels.

Skippy® Dippin'

1 cup **Cook Time: 30 seconds**

1 cup Skippy® Peanut Butter

1. In small microwavae-safe bowl, microwave Skippy® Peanut Butter at HIGH 30 seconds or until Peanut Butter is melted and smooth, stirring once.

Serving Suggestion Use as a dip for fruit and other treats or spoon over ice cream.

Peanut Butter Celery Sticks

6 servings Prep Time: 10 minutes

¼ cup Skippy® Peanut Butter

3 ribs celery

¼ cup mini pretzel sticks or raisins

1. Evenly spread Skippy® Peanut Butter down the center of each rib of celery; top with pretzel sticks.

2. To serve, cut each rib of celery into 4 pieces.

Peanut Butter S'mores

1 serving **Prep Time: *5 minutes***

1 Tbsp. Skippy® Peanut Butter

4 graham cracker squares

2 large marshmallows

2 slices banana

1. Evenly spread Skippy® Peanut Butter on 2 graham cracker squares.
2. On microwave-safe plate, arrange crackers, then top each with marshmallows.
3. Microwave at HIGH 15 seconds or until marshmallows puff.
4. Top each with banana slice, then remaining graham cracker squares.

Peanut Butter 'N Fruit S'mores

4 servings **Prep Time: *5 minutes***

¼ cup Skippy® Peanut Butter

4 graham crackers

½ cup finely chopped apple, banana, strawberries or grapes

¼ cup semi-sweet chocolate chips

8 large marshmallows or ½ cup mini marshmallows

1. Evenly spread Skippy® Peanut Butter on graham crackers.
2. On microwave-safe plate, arrange crackers, then top with remaining ingredients.
3. Microwave at HIGH 20 seconds or until marshmallows puff.

Peanut Butter S'mores

Peanut Butter Snack Mix

about 10 cups Prep Time: *15 minutes* Cook Time: *10 minutes*

1 cup Skippy® Creamy Peanut Butter

2 Tbsp. honey

5 to 6 cups toasted corn cereal squares or crispy
rice cereal

3 to 4 cups pretzels, sesame sticks and/or cheddar
flavored fish or crackers

½ cup dry-roasted unsalted peanuts and/or sunflower
seeds (optional)

½ cup raisins or dried fruit mix

½ cup semi-sweet chocolate chips

1. Preheat oven to 325°F.

2. In small microwave-safe bowl, microwave Skippy®
Creamy Peanut Butter and honey at HIGH 45 seconds
or until Peanut Butter is melted. Stir and set aside.

3. In large bowl, combine cereal, pretzels and peanuts.
Pour melted peanut butter mixture over cereal mixture;
toss to coat. On foil-lined baking sheet, evenly spread
cereal mixture.

4. Bake 10 minutes, stirring once. On wire rack, cool
completely. Stir in raisins and chocolate. Store in
airtight container or plastic storage bags.

Peanut Butter Popcorn

10 servings Prep Time: *5 minutes*

½ cup Skippy® Peanut Butter

1 Tbsp. honey

1 bag (3.5 oz.) microwave popcorn, cooked according to
package directions (about 10 cups popped popcorn)

1. In large microwave-safe bowl, microwave Skippy®
Peanut Butter at HIGH 40 seconds or until melted;
stir in honey.

2. Add popcorn and toss until evenly coated.

Peanut Butter Cereal Treats

36 servings Prep Time: *5 minutes* Cook Time: *2 minutes*
Chill Time: *15 minutes*

4 cups crispy rice cereal

½ cup sugar

½ cup light or dark corn syrup

½ cup Skippy® Creamy Peanut Butter

1. Line 8- or 9-inch square baking pan with plastic wrap. In large bowl, pour cereal; set aside.

2. In medium saucepan, bring sugar and corn syrup to a boil over medium heat, stirring occasionally. Boil 1 minute, then remove from heat.

3. Stir in Skippy® Creamy Peanut Butter until smooth. Pour over cereal; stir to coat. Press evenly into prepared pan.

4. On cutting board, let cool 15 minutes; remove from pan, then remove plastic wrap. Cut into squares to serve.

Tip Slip a plastic bag over your hand before pressing mixture into pan so the cereal doesn't stick to your hand.

Slammin' Graham Cracker Stacks

2 servings **Prep Time:** *5 minutes*

8 graham cracker squares

¼ cup Skippy® Peanut Butter, melted

¼ cup grape, strawberry or raspberry jelly, warmed

½ cup chopped apples, bananas, raisins or nuts

1. On serving plate, arrange graham crackers.

2. Drizzle with melted Skippy® Peanut Butter and warm jelly, then top with apples.

Peanut Chocolate Graham Squares

12 servings **Prep Time:** *10 minutes* **Cook Time:** *1 minute*

3 cups mini marshmallows

½ cup Skippy® Super Chunk® Peanut Butter

2 Tbsp. margarine

24 graham cracker squares

¼ cup mini semi-sweet chocolate chips

1. In medium microwave-safe bowl, microwave marshmallows, Skippy® Super Chunk® Peanut Butter and margarine at HIGH, stirring occasionally, 1 minute or until melted; cool slightly.

2. On 12 crackers, spread about 2 tablespoons peanut butter mixture, then top with remaining crackers. Press lightly until filling is even with edge of crackers.

3. Dip edges in chocolate chips. Serve immediately or let set.

Slammin' Graham Cracker Stacks

Frogs on a Lily pad

5 servings **Prep Time:** *5 minutes*

5 dried apricots
Skippy® Peanut Butter
5 walnut halves

1. Slice apricots in half lengthwise to make two circles. Spread Skippy® Peanut Butter on 5 halves, then top with remaining apricot halves.

2. Spread tops with additional Skippy® Peanut Butter, then top with walnuts.

Skippy® Parfait

4 servings **Prep Time:** *10 minutes*

1 box (3.9 oz.) vanilla or chocolate instant pudding mix, prepared according to package directions
½ cup Skippy® Peanut Butter
2 Skippy™ Snack Bars, any variety, chopped

1. With wire whisk, blend prepared pudding with Skippy® Peanut Butter. Evenly spoon mixture into dessert dishes.

2. Just before serving, top with Skippy™ Snack Bars.

Peanut Butter & Jelly Cupcakes

24 servings Prep Time: 15 minutes Cook Time: 20 minutes

1 box (1 lb. 2.25 oz.) yellow cake mix (non-pudding type)

1 cup Skippy® Creamy Peanut Butter

½ cup grape, strawberry or raspberry jelly

Chocolate frosting (optional)

1. Preheat oven to 350°F. Line 24-cup muffin pan with paper cupcake liners; set aside.

2. In large bowl, with electric mixer on medium speed, beat cake mix and Skippy® Creamy Peanut Butter until coarse crumbs form. Continue preparing cake mix according to package directions, omitting oil.

3. Evenly spoon batter into prepared pan, filling each only half full. Top each with 1 teaspoon jelly, then carefully top with remaining batter.

4. Bake 20 minutes or until toothpick inserted in centers comes out clean. On wire rack, cool for 10 minutes; remove from pan and cool completely. Spread with frosting.

Extra Special Peanut Butter Cereal Treats

24 servings Prep Time: *15 minutes* Cook Time: *2 minutes*
Chill Time: *20 minutes*

6 cups crispy rice cereal or toasted corn cereal squares

4 cups mini marshmallows

¾ cup sugar

¾ cup light or dark corn syrup

1 cup Skippy® Creamy Peanut Butter

½ cup semi-sweet chocolate chips

1. Spray 13 x 9-inch baking pan with nonstick cooking spray; set aside.

2. In large bowl, combine cereal and 2 cups marshmallows; set aside.

3. In 2-quart saucepan, bring sugar and corn syrup to a boil, stirring occasionally.

4. Boil 1 minute, then remove from heat. Stir in Skippy® Creamy Peanut Butter until smooth.

5. Pour peanut butter mixture over cereal; stir to coat. Evenly press into prepared pan. Top with chocolate, then remaining 2 cups marshmallows.

6. Broil 10 seconds or until tops of marshmallows are golden; let cool. To serve, cut into squares.

Savory Sensations

CHAPTER FIVE

Creamy Peanut Vinaigrette Dressing

1 cup dressing Prep Time: *10 minutes*

⅓ cup Skippy® Creamy Peanut Butter

¼ cup chicken broth

3 Tbsp. rice wine vinegar

2 Tbsp. olive oil

1 Tbsp. firmly packed brown sugar

2 tsp. lime juice

⅛ tsp. salt

1. In food processor or blender, process all ingredients about 1 minute or until smooth.

2. Store in airtight container in refrigerator until ready to serve.

Serving Suggestion Serve over mixed salad greens.

Creamy Peanut-Garlic Dressing

about 1 cup dressing Prep Time: *10 minutes*

⅓ cup Skippy® Creamy Peanut Butter

¼ cup rice wine vinegar

¼ cup olive oil

¼ cup chicken broth

2 Tbsp. firmly packed brown sugar

1 medium clove garlic, peeled

1 tsp. soy sauce

Red pepper flakes (optional)

1. In food processor or blender, process all ingredients about 1 minute or until smooth.

2. Store in airtight container in refrigerator until ready to serve.

Serving Suggestion Serve over mixed salad greens.

Creamy Peanut Vinaigrette Dressing

Oriental Chicken 'N Noodle Salad

4 servings **Prep Time:** *15 minutes* **Cook Time:** *6 minutes*

8 ounces angel hair pasta or vermicelli

1 lb. boneless, skinless chicken breasts

¾ cup PLUS 2 Tbsp. Italian salad dressing

¾ cup sliced green onions

2 Tbsp. finely chopped fresh ginger*

¼ cup finely chopped cilantro or parsley

2 Tbsp. Skippy® Creamy Peanut Butter

2 Tbsp. firmly packed brown sugar

1 Tbsp. soy sauce

1 Tbsp. sherry

¼ tsp. red pepper flakes

2 medium carrots, sliced

1 medium red bell pepper, chopped

1. Cook pasta according to package directions; drain and rinse with cold water until completely cool.

2. On broiler pan, arrange chicken. Brush with 2 tablespoons dressing, then broil, turning once, 6 minutes or until chicken is thoroughly cooked.

3. Meanwhile, in 12-inch skillet, heat remaining ¾ cup dressing and cook green onions and ginger over medium-high heat, stirring occasionally, 2 minutes or until tender. Stir in cilantro, Skippy® Creamy Peanut Butter, brown sugar, soy sauce, sherry and red pepper flakes.

4. In large bowl, toss pasta with green onion mixture, carrots and red pepper. To serve, arrange on platter, then top with sliced chicken. Garnish, if desired, with additional sliced green onions.

*SUBSTITUTION: Use ½ teaspoon ground ginger and decrease red pepper flakes to ⅛ teaspoon.

Peanut Coconut Thai Soup

7 servings Prep Time: 10 minutes Cook Time: 12 minutes

2 Tbsp. margarine

4 ounces shiitake, crimini, or white mushrooms, sliced

¼ cup Skippy® Creamy Peanut Butter

4 cups chicken broth

1 can (14 oz.) coconut milk

1 Tbsp. rice wine vinegar

2 tsp. soy sauce

¾ tsp. salt

½ tsp. ground ginger (optional)

¼ cup chopped fresh cilantro

1. In 5-quart saucepot, melt margarine on medium-high heat and cook mushrooms stirring occasionally, 4 minutes.
2. Add Skippy® Creamy Peanut Butter, broth, coconut milk, vinegar, soy sauce, salt and ginger. Bring to a boil over medium-high heat, stirring occasionally with wire whisk.
3. Reduce heat to low and simmer 5 minutes. Just before serving, stir in cilantro.

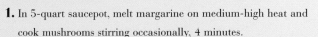

Savory Sensations

Thai Peanut Chicken & Noodles

4 servings Prep Time: *5 minutes* Cook Time: *20 minutes*

2 Tbsp. vegetable oil

1 lb. boneless, skinless chicken breasts or thighs, cut into ½-inch pieces

2 cloves garlic, finely chopped

1 medium green or red bell pepper, sliced

1½ cups chicken broth

⅓ cup Skippy® Creamy or Super Chunk® Peanut Butter

3 Tbsp. soy sauce

2 Tbsp. honey

1 Tbsp. cornstarch

1 Tbsp. rice wine vinegar

2 tsp. finely chopped fresh ginger

½ tsp. red pepper flakes (or to taste)

2 green onions, sliced

½ lb. Asian noodles, spaghetti or linguine, cooked and drained

Serving Suggestion Garnish, if desired, with chopped peanuts and chopped fresh cilantro.

1. In 12-inch nonstick skillet, heat 1 tablespoon oil over medium-high heat and cook chicken, stirring occasionally, until chicken is thoroughly cooked, about 7 minutes. Remove chicken and set aside.
2. In same skillet, heat remaining 1 tablespoon oil over medium-high heat and cook garlic and green pepper, stirring occasionally, 2 minutes.
3. Add chicken broth, Skippy® Creamy Peanut Butter, soy sauce, honey, cornstarch, vinegar and ginger. Cook, stirring frequently, until sauce is thickened and smooth, about 2 minutes.
4. Return chicken to skillet. Stir in green onion and simmer until heated through, about 3 minutes. Serve over hot noodles.

Warm Peanut-Sesame Noodles

4 servings Prep Time: *20 minutes* Cook Time: *5 minutes*

½ cup Skippy® Creamy or Super Chunk® Peanut Butter

2 Tbsp. firmly packed brown sugar

1 tsp. toasted sesame seeds (optional)

½ tsp. ground ginger

½ cup water

2 Tbsp. rice wine vinegar

2 Tbsp. soy sauce

1 Tbsp. peanut or vegetable oil

8 ounces spaghetti, cooked and drained

1. In 1-quart saucepan, combine all ingredients except spaghetti. Bring to a boil on medium heat, stirring constantly.

2. Reduce heat to low and simmer, stirring frequently, 1 minute.

3. Immediately toss with hot spaghetti.

Serving Suggestion Garnish, if desired, with chopped green onions.

Chicken Sate with Peanut Sauce

8 servings **Prep Time: *10 minutes* Marinate Time: *3 hours***
Cook Time: *6 minutes*

¼ cup olive oil

2 Tbsp. soy sauce

2 Tbsp. apple cider vinegar

2 Tbsp. sugar

2 tsp. grated fresh ginger

2 cloves garlic, finely chopped

2 lbs. boneless, skinless chicken breast halves, cut in thin strips

Peanut Sauce*

Peanut Sauce*

2 Tbsp. olive oil

1 small onion, finely chopped

2 cloves garlic, finely chopped

½ tsp. red pepper flakes

⅔ cup Skippy® Creamy or Super Chunk® Peanut Butter

2 Tbsp. firmly packed brown sugar

2 Tbsp. soy sauce

2 Tbsp. apple cider vinegar

1 to 2 tsp. grated fresh ginger

1 cup water

1. For marinade, in blender, blend all ingredients except chicken and Peanut Sauce.

2. In large, shallow nonaluminum baking dish or plastic bag, pour marinade over chicken; turn to coat. Cover, or close bag, and marinate in refrigerator, turning occasionally, 3 hours.

3. Remove chicken from marinade, discarding marinade. On skewers, thread chicken.

4. Grill or broil chicken, turning occasionally, 6 minutes or until chicken is thoroughly cooked. Serve with Peanut Sauce.

*Peanut Sauce

1. In small saucepan, heat olive oil over medium heat and cook onion, garlic and red pepper flakes, stirring frequently, 3 minutes or until onion is tender.

2. Stir in Skippy® Creamy Peanut Butter, brown sugar, soy sauce, vinegar and ginger. Gradually stir in water until blended. Serve warm.

Peanut-Sesame BBQ Sauce

4 servings Prep Time: 10 minutes Cook Time: 14 minutes

½ cup Skippy® Creamy or Super Chunk® Peanut Butter

2 Tbsp. firmly packed brown sugar

1 tsp. toasted sesame seeds (optional)

½ tsp. ground ginger

½ cup water

¼ cup red wine vinegar or apple cider vinegar

2 Tbsp. soy sauce

1 Tbsp. peanut or vegetable oil

4 boneless, skinless chicken breast halves, (about 1¼ lbs.)

1. In 1-quart saucepan, combine all ingredients except chicken. Bring to a boil over medium heat, stirring constantly, for 1 minute.

2. Reduce heat to low and simmer, stirring frequently, 1 minute.

3. Grill or broil chicken, turning and brushing occasionally with ½ cup peanut-sesame sauce, 12 minutes or until chicken is thoroughly cooked. Serve with remaining sauce.

Variation Try substituting pork chops or steak for chicken.

Beef Thai-style Rice Bowl

2 servings Prep Time: 25 minutes Cook Time: 6 minutes

⅓ cup water

¼ cup Skippy® Creamy Peanut Butter

1 Tbsp. soy sauce

1½ cups extra meaty pasta sauce

⅓ cup frozen green peas

1 tsp. chopped green onions

½ tsp. hot curry powder

2 cups hot cooked rice

1. In 2-quart saucepan, cook water, Skippy® Creamy Peanut Butter and soy sauce, on medium heat, stirring constantly, until Peanut Butter is melted.

2. Stir in pasta sauce, peas, green onions and curry powder. Bring to a boil over high heat.

3. Reduce heat to low and simmer, stirring occasionally, 5 minutes or until peas are heated through.

4. To serve, evenly spoon rice into two bowls, then evenly top with hot sauce mixture.

Serving Suggestion Garnish, if desired, with chopped peanuts and finely chopped fresh cilantro.

Savory Sensations

Chicken with Savory Peanut-Sesame BBQ Sauce

African Beef Stew

8 servings Prep Time: *10 minutes* Cook Time: *1 hour 15 minutes*

3 Tbsp. olive oil

1½ lbs. beef stew meat, cut into 1-inch cubes

1 large onion, chopped

2 cloves garlic, finely chopped

1 can (28 oz.) whole peeled tomatoes, undrained

1 cup beef broth

½ cup Skippy® Peanut Butter

1 tsp. ground cumin (optional)

1. In 6-quart saucepot, heat 1 tablespoon olive oil on medium-high heat and brown ½ of the meat; remove meat and set aside. Repeat with an additional 1 tablespoon olive oil and remaining meat; remove meat and set aside.

2. In same saucepot, heat remaining 1 tablespoon olive oil on medium-high heat and cook onion, stirring occasionally, 3 minutes. Add garlic and cook 30 seconds.

3. Stir in tomatoes, broth, Skippy® Peanut Butter and cumin. Bring to a boil over high heat.

4. Reduce heat to low and return beef to saucepot. Simmer covered, stirring occasionally, 1 hour or until beef is tender. Season, if desired, with salt and ground black pepper.

Tip Try serving over hot cooked rice or noodles and garnish, if desired, with chopped cilantro.

Peanut-glazed Steak

4 servings Prep Time: *15 minutes* Cook Time: *8 minutes*

2 Tbsp. margarine

1 small onion, thinly sliced

1 lb. boneless beef top sirloin steak, thinly sliced

¼ cup Skippy® Creamy Peanut Butter

1 Tbsp. firmly packed brown sugar

½ tsp. red pepper flakes

¼ cup beef broth

½ tsp. soy sauce

1. In 12-inch nonstick skillet, melt margarine over medium-high heat and cook onion, stirring occasionally, 3 minutes.

2. Add steak and cook, stirring occasionally, 3 minutes or until desired doneness.

3. Reduce heat to medium and stir in remaining ingredients. Cook, stirring constantly, 1 minute or until sauce is blended and steak is glazed.

Serving Suggestion Serve, if desired, over shredded lettuce with chopped tomatoes and cucumbers or over hot cooked rice. Garnish, if desired, with lime wedges.

Grilled Beef Satay with Spicy Peanut Sauce

4 servings **Prep Time: *20 minutes*** **Marinate Time: *2 hours***
Cook Time: *2 minutes*

1 lb. beef top round steak, about 1-inch-thick

1 cup Italian salad dressing

1 Tbsp. firmly packed brown sugar

1 Tbsp. finely chopped fresh cilantro

1 Tbsp. finely chopped fresh ginger

½ cup Skippy® Creamy Peanut Butter

¼ tsp. hot or mild curry powder

¼ tsp. ground red pepper

Cucumber Relish (optional)*

Cucumber Relish*

1 large cucumber, peeled, seeded and diced

⅓ cup finely chopped red onion

¼ cup Italian salad dressing

1 Tbsp. finely chopped fresh cilantro

1. Cut steak into ⅛-inch strips; set aside.

2. For marinade, blend ½ cup dressing, brown sugar, cilantro and ginger. In large, shallow nonaluminum baking dish or plastic bag, pour ¼ cup marinade over steak; turn to coat.

3. Cover, or close bag, and marinate in refrigerator, turning occasionally, 2 hours. Refrigerate remaining marinade.

4. Meanwhile for peanut sauce, in small bowl, blend Skippy® Creamy Peanut Butter, remaining ½ cup dressing, curry and red pepper; set aside.

5. Remove steak from marinade, discarding marinade. On skewers, thread steak.

6. Grill steak, turning once and brushing frequently with refrigerated marinade, 2 minutes or until steak is desired doneness. Serve with Peanut Sauce and, if desired, Cucumber Relish.

*Cucumber Relish

1. In small bowl, combine all ingredients; chill until ready to serve.

4 servings Prep Time: *15 minutes* Marinate Time: *10 minutes*
Cook Time: *10 minutes*

1 lb. uncooked large shrimp, peeled and deveined

2 Tbsp. lime juice

4 Tbsp. margarine

2 cloves garlic, thinly sliced

⅔ cup chicken broth

⅓ cup Skippy® Creamy Peanut Butter

2 Tbsp. firmly packed brown sugar

Hot cooked rice

1. In medium bowl, toss shrimp with lime juice. Season, if desired, with salt. Marinate for 10 minutes.

2. In 12-inch nonstick skillet, melt 2 tablespoons margarine over medium-high heat and cook shrimp, turning occasionally, 2 minutes or until shrimp turn pink.

3. Add garlic and cook 30 seconds; remove shrimp and keep warm.

4. In same skillet, add remaining 2 tablespoons margarine. Stir in broth, Skippy® Creamy Peanut Butter and brown sugar. Bring to a boil over medium heat, stirring constantly with wire whisk, until thickened.

5. To serve, arrange shrimp over hot rice and drizzle with peanut sauce.

Serving Suggestion
Garnish, if desired, with toasted coconut.

Cookie Creations

CHAPTER SIX

Skippy® Oatmeal Applesauce Cookies

3 dozen cookies Prep Time: *10 minutes* Cook Time: *15 minutes*

1½ cups quick cooking oats

1 cup all-purpose flour

½ tsp. baking soda

½ cup margarine

¾ cup Skippy® Creamy or Super Chunk® Peanut Butter

¾ cup firmly packed brown sugar

1 large egg

½ tsp. vanilla extract

1 cup applesauce

½ cup raisins (optional)

1. Preheat oven to 350°F. In small bowl, combine oats, flour and baking soda; set aside.

2. In large bowl, with electric mixer on medium speed, beat margarine and Skippy® Creamy Peanut Butter until smooth. Beat in brown sugar, then egg, vanilla and applesauce until blended. Beat in flour mixture just until blended, then stir in raisins.

3. On ungreased baking sheets, drop dough by rounded tablespoonfuls, 2-inches apart. Dough will be loose.

4. Bake 15 minutes or until golden. Remove cookies to wire rack and cool completely.

Best Ever Peanut Butter-Oatmeal Cookies

6 dozen cookies Prep Time: *20 minutes* Cook Time: *13 minutes*

2 cups quick cooking oats, uncooked

2 cups all-purpose flour

1 tsp. baking powder

1 tsp. baking soda

¼ tsp. salt

1 cup margarine

1 cup Skippy® Creamy or Super Chunk® Peanut Butter

1 cup granulated sugar

1 cup firmly packed brown sugar

2 eggs

2 tsp. vanilla extract

1 package (12 oz.) semi-sweet chocolate chips (optional)

1. Preheat oven to 350°F.

2. In small bowl, combine oats, flour, baking powder, baking soda and salt; set aside.

3. In large bowl, with electric mixer on medium speed, beat margarine and Skippy® Creamy Peanut Butter until smooth.

4. Beat in sugars, then eggs and vanilla until blended. Beat in flour mixture just until blended, then stir in chocolate.

5. On ungreased baking sheets, drop dough by rounded tablespoonfuls, 2-inches apart.

6. Bake 13 minutes or until golden. Remove cookies to wire rack and cool completely.

Cookie Creations

Chewy Peanut Butter Cereal Cookies

5 dozen cookies Prep Time: *15 minutes* Cook Time: *12 minutes*

1¼ cups all-purpose flour

1 tsp. baking powder

1 tsp. baking soda

¼ tsp. salt

1 cup Skippy® Creamy or Super Chunk® Peanut Butter

1 cup margarine

1 cup granulated sugar

1 cup firmly packed brown sugar

2 eggs

1 tsp. vanilla extract

6 cups crispy rice cereal or toasted corn cereal squares

1. Preheat oven to 350°F.
2. In small bowl, combine flour, baking powder, baking soda and salt; set aside.
3. In large bowl, with electric mixer on medium speed, beat Skippy® Creamy Peanut Butter and margarine until smooth.
4. Beat in sugars, then eggs and vanilla until blended. Beat in flour mixture, then stir in cereal.
5. On ungreased baking sheets, drop dough by rounded tablespoonfuls, 2-inches apart. If desired, press one additional cereal square in center of each cookie.
6. Bake 12 minutes or until golden. On wire rack, let stand for 2 minutes; remove from sheets and cool completely.

Honey Bear Cookies

1½ cups quick cooking oats

1 cup all-purpose flour

½ tsp. baking soda

½ cup margarine

½ cup Skippy® Creamy Peanut Butter

½ cup honey

1 large egg

½ tsp. vanilla extract

½ cup raisins (optional)

1. Preheat oven to 350°F. In small bowl, combine oats, flour and baking soda; set aside.
2. In large bowl, with electric mixer on medium speed, beat margarine and Skippy® Creamy Peanut Butter until smooth. Beat in honey, egg and vanilla until blended. Beat in flour mixture just until blended, then stir in raisins.
3. On ungreased baking sheets, drop dough by rounded tablespoonfuls, 2-inches apart.
4. Bake 13 minutes or until golden. Remove cookies to wire rack and cool completely.

Crisp Peanut Butter Cookies

6 dozen cookies **Prep Time:** *20 minutes* **Cook Time:** *12 minutes*

2½ cups all-purpose flour

1 tsp. baking powder

1 tsp. baking soda

¼ tsp. salt

1 cup Skippy® Creamy or Super Chunk® Peanut Butter

1 cup margarine

1 cup granulated sugar

1 cup firmly packed brown sugar

2 eggs

1 tsp. vanilla extract

1. Preheat oven to 350°F.

2. In small bowl, combine flour, baking powder, baking soda and salt; set aside.

3. In large bowl, with electric mixer, beat Skippy® Creamy Peanut Butter and margarine until smooth.

4. Beat in sugars, then eggs and vanilla until blended. Beat in flour mixture just until blended. (If necessary, refrigerate dough until easy to handle.)

5. Shape dough into 1-inch balls. On ungreased baking sheets, arrange balls 2-inches apart. With fork dipped in sugar, gently flatten each cookie and press crisscross pattern into tops.

6. Bake 12 minutes or until lightly golden. On wire rack, cool completely. Store in tightly covered container.

Cookie Creations

88

Skippy® Truffle Cookies

4½ dozen cookies Prep Time: *15 minutes* Cook Time: *9 minutes*

A flourless cookie... with a decadent truffle-like texture

1 cup Skippy® Creamy Peanut Butter

1 cup firmly packed light brown sugar

1 large egg

1 tsp. baking soda

½ cup semi-sweet chocolate chips

1. Preheat oven to 350°F.

2. In small bowl, with wooden spoon, combine all ingredients except chocalate until blended. Stir in chocolate just until combined.

3. On ungreased baking sheets, using slightly rounded teaspoonfuls, drop dough 2-inches apart (Do not flatten)

4. Bake 9 minutes or until cookies are puffed and golden. (Cookies will be very soft) On wire rack, place baking sheets and let stand for 5 minutes.

5. Remove cookies from sheets and cool completely.

Peanut Butter & Jelly Cookie Squares

about 1 dozen cookies Prep Time: *15 minutes* Cook Time: *35 minutes*

2¼ cups all-purpose flour

½ cup Skippy® Creamy Peanut Butter

½ cup margarine

½ cup firmly packed brown sugar

¼ cup granulated sugar

1 egg

1 cup strawberry, grape or raspberry jelly

1. Preheat oven to 350°F. Spray 13 x 9-inch baking pan with nonstick cooking spray; set aside.

2. In large bowl, with electric mixer on medium speed, beat all ingredients except jelly for 2 minutes or until crumbly. Reserve 1 cup peanut butter mixture.

3. Spread remaining peanut butter mixture into prepared pan. Spread on jelly, then crumble reserved peanut butter mixture on top.

4. Bake 35 minutes or until golden. On wire rack, cool completely. To serve, cut into squares.

Peanut Butter & Jelly Thumbprint Cookies

4 dozen cookies **Prep Time:** *15 minutes* **Chill Time:** *1 hour*
Cook Time: *5 minutes*

3 cups all-purpose flour
1½ tsp. baking powder
½ tsp. salt
1 cup margarine
½ cup granulated sugar
½ cup firmly packed light brown sugar
½ cup Skippy® Creamy Peanut Butter
1 egg
1½ tsp. vanilla extract
¼ cup grape jelly

1. In medium bowl, combine flour, baking powder and salt; set aside.
2. In large bowl, with electric mixer, beat margarine, sugars and Skippy® Creamy Peanut Butter until light and fluffy, about 3 minutes.
3. Beat in egg and vanilla, scraping sides occasionally. Gradually beat in flour mixture until blended. Wrap dough in plastic wrap and freeze at least 1 hour.
4. Preheat oven to 425°F. On ungreased baking sheets, shape by tablespoonfuls into balls and arrange.
5. With thumb or rounded ¼ teaspoon measure, make indentation in center of each cookie; fill each with ¼ teaspoon jelly.
6. Bake 5 minutes or until bottoms of cookies are lightly golden. On wire rack, cool completely.

Cookie Creations

Peanut Butter & Jelly Sandwich Cookies

4 dozen cookies Prep Time: *15 minutes* Cook Time: *5 minutes*
Chill Time: *1 hour*

3 cups all-purpose flour

1½ tsp. baking powder

½ tsp. salt

1 cup margarine

½ cup granulated sugar

½ cup firmly packed light brown sugar

½ cup Skippy® Creamy Peanut Butter

1 egg

1½ tsp. vanilla extract

¼ cup your favorite jelly

1. In medium bowl, combine flour, baking powder and salt; set aside.

2. In large bowl, with electric mixer, beat margarine, sugars and Skippy® Creamy Peanut Butter until light and fluffy, about 3 minutes.

3. Beat in egg and vanilla, scraping sides occasionally. Gradually beat in flour mixture until blended. Divide dough into four equal pieces. Shape into logs, each 2-inches wide. Wrap in plastic wrap and freeze at least 1 hour.

4. Preheat oven to 425°F. Slice logs into ¼-inch slices and arrange on ungreased baking sheets. With fork, lightly pierce tops.

5. Bake 5 minutes or until bottoms are lightly golden. On wire rack, cool completely.

6. Spread ¼ teaspoon jelly on flat side of one cookie. Press together with another cookie to form sandwich. Repeat with remaining cookies and jelly.

Variation

For Peanut Butter Cookie Ice Cream Sandwiches, substitute 2 tablespoons vanilla ice cream or frozen yogurt for jelly. Roll ice cream edges in semi-sweet chocolate mini chips, then freeze until firm.

6 dozen cookies Prep Time: *20 minutes* Cook Time: *13 minutes*

2½ cups quick-cooking oats

1¼ cups all-purpose flour

1 tsp. baking powder

1 tsp. baking soda

¼ tsp. salt

1 cup Skippy® Creamy or Super Chunk® Peanut Butter

1 cup margarine

1 cup granulated sugar

1 cup firmly packed brown sugar

2 eggs

2 tsp. vanilla extract

72 chocolate candy kisses

1. Preheat oven to 350°F.

2. In small bowl, combine oats, flour, baking powder, baking soda and salt; set aside.

3. In large bowl, with electric mixer on medium speed, beat Skippy® Creamy Peanut Butter and margarine until smooth.

4. Beat in sugars, then eggs and vanilla until blended. Beat in flour mixture just until blended.

5. On ungreased baking sheets, drop dough by level tablespoonfuls, 2-inches apart.

6. Bake 13 minutes or until golden. Immediately press chocolate kiss firmly in center of each cookie. Remove cookies to wire rack and cool completely.

Cookie Creations

94

Skippy® Holiday Peanut Butter Cookies

5 dozen cookies Prep Time: *20 minutes* Chill Time: *1 hour* Cook Time: *8 minutes*

½ cup Skippy® Creamy Peanut Butter

½ cup margarine

½ cup firmly packed brown sugar

½ cup granulated sugar

1 egg

½ tsp. vanilla extract

1½ cups all-purpose flour

¾ tsp. baking soda

½ tsp. baking powder

¼ tsp. salt

1. In large bowl, with electric mixer, beat Skippy® Creamy Peanut Butter, margarine, sugars, egg and vanilla at medium speed until smooth.
2. Beat in remaining ingredients at low speed just until blended. Divide dough in half. Chill about 1 hour.
3. Preheat oven to 375°F.
4. On well-floured board with well-floured rolling pin, roll each dough half about ⅛ inch thick. With cookie cutters, cut dough into circles or shapes. Arrange on ungreased cookie sheets.
5. Bake 8 minutes or until lightly golden. Let stand on cookie sheets for 2 minutes. Remove from sheets and cool completely on wire racks. Reroll dough trimmings to cut additional cookies; bake.

Serving Suggestion Decorate with icing, decorative sprinkles and candies as desired.

Desserts & More

CHAPTER SEVEN

2 servings **Prep Time:** *5 minutes*

1 pint (16 oz.) chocolate or vanilla ice cream
½ cup Skippy® Creamy Peanut Butter
¼ cup milk*

1. In blender, process all ingredients until smooth. Serve immediately.

Tip *Use more milk for a thinner consistency, if desired.

Dreamy Banana Shake

2 servings **Prep Time:** *5 minutes*

1 pint (16 oz.) chocolate or vanilla ice cream
½ cup Skippy® Creamy Peanut Butter
½ cup milk
1 medium banana

1. In blender, process all ingredients until smooth. Serve immediately.

Desserts & More

Fluffy Peanut Butter Frosting

about 2 cups **Prep Time:** *10 minutes*

1 jar (7oz.) marshmallow cream

½ cup Skippy® Creamy Peanut Butter

⅓ cup margarine

1⅓ cups confectioners sugar

2 Tbsp. milk

¼ tsp. vanilla extract

1. In small bowl, with electric mixer on low speed, beat marshmallow cream, Skippy® Creamy Peanut Butter and margarine until smooth.

2. Increase speed to medium and beat in remaining ingredients until blended.

Serving Suggestion Use to frost cupcakes or your favorite chocolate cake.

Peanut Butter 'N Chocolate Dip

20 servings Cook Time: *2 minutes*

1 cup Skippy® Creamy Peanut Butter
1 cup semi-sweet chocolate chips
Your favorite dippers (such as pretzels, bananas, marshmallows, strawberries or shortbread cookies)

1. In medium microwave-safe bowl, microwave ½ cup Skippy® Creamy Peanut Butter and chocolate at HIGH, stirring occasionally, 1½ minutes or until mixture is melted and smooth.
2. Dip dippers in peanut butter mixture, then let stand on waxed-paper-lined baking sheets until chocolate is set, about 30 minutes.
3. In small microwave-safe bowl, microwave remaining ½ cup Peanut Butter at HIGH 30 seconds or until melted. Stir, then drizzle over dippers.

Peanut Butter Pie Bars

32 servings Prep Time: *15 minutes* Cook Time: *35 minutes*

Crust:

2 cups all-purpose flour

⅓ cup sugar

½ lb. margarine

¼ tsp. salt

Filling:

2 eggs

¾ cup light or dark corn syrup

½ cup sugar

½ cup Skippy® Creamy Peanut Butter

2 Tbsp. margarine, melted

1 tsp. vanilla extract

¾ cup dry roasted peanuts

1. Preheat oven to 350°F.

2. For crust, in large bowl with electric mixer, beat flour, sugar, margarine and salt until mixture resembles coarse crumbs.

3. In 13 x 9-inch baking pan coated with nonstick cooking spray, firmly press crumbs into bottom of and ¼ inch up sides. Bake 15 minutes or until crust is golden brown.

4. For filling, in large bowl, beat eggs, corn syrup, sugar, Skippy® Creamy Peanut Butter, margarine and vanilla until well blended. Stir in peanuts.

5. Evenly pour mixture over hot crust. Bake 20 minutes or until filling is firm around edges and slightly firm in center. On wire rack, cool completely. To serve, cut into bars.

1½ cups all-purpose flour

1 tsp. baking powder

1 tsp. salt

⅔ cup margarine, softened

2 cups sugar

4 eggs

1 cup semi-sweet chocolate chips, melted

½ cup Skippy® Creamy Peanut Butter

1. Preheat oven to 350°F. Grease 13 x 9-inch baking pan; set aside.

2. In medium bowl, combine flour, baking powder and salt; set aside.

3. In large bowl, with electric mixer, beat margarine and sugar on medium-high speed until light and fluffy, about 5 minutes.

4. Beat in eggs, scraping sides occasionally. Gradually beat in flour mixture until blended.

5. Remove 2 cups batter to medium bowl and stir in melted chocolate. Evenly spread chocolate batter into prepared pan.

6. Add Skippy® Creamy Peanut Butter to remaining batter in large bowl; beat until blended. Spoon over chocolate batter and spread evenly.

7. Bake 35 minutes or until center is set. On wire rack, cool completely. To serve, cut into bars.

Frozen Peanutty Pops

6 servings Prep Time: 10 minutes Chill Time: 4 hours

½ cup Skippy® Peanut Butter

2 cups milk

1 package (3.9 oz.) chocolate or vanilla instant pudding mix

1. In medium bowl, with wire whisk, blend all ingredients. Spoon pudding into 4-oz. waxed paper cups or into muffin pan lined with cupcake liners.
2. Place plastic spoons or popsicle sticks in center of each and freeze for 4 hours or until firm.
3. To serve, peel off paper cups.

Gooey Peanut Butter S'more Brownies

24 servings Prep Time: 15 minutes Cook Time: 30 minutes

1 box (19.8 oz.) brownie mix

1 jar (7 oz.) marshmallow cream

1 cup creamy chocolate frosting

1 cup Skippy® Peanut Butter

1. Prepare, bake, and cool brownie mix according to package directions for 13 x 9-inch baking pan.
2. With spoon, evenly drop marshmallow cream onto cooled brownies.
3. In small microwave-safe bowl, microwave frosting at HIGH 30 seconds or until melted and smooth. Repeat with Skippy® Peanut Butter.
4. Pour melted frosting, then melted Peanut Butter over marshmallow cream and swirl with butter knife to marble. Let cool completely. To serve, cut into squares.

Frozen Peanutty Pops

Desserts & More

4 servings Prep Time: *5 minutes* Cook Time: *15 minutes*

1 can (10 oz.) refrigerated pizza crust
½ cup Skippy® Peanut Butter
1 medium banana, sliced into ½-inch pieces
Your favorite vanilla or fruit yogurt

1. Preheat oven to 400°F. On greased baking sheet, unroll crust and press into a 12 x 14-inch rectangle.

3. Evenly spread Skippy® Peanut Butter lengthwise over ½ of the crust leaving a ½-inch border around edges, then top with bananas.

4. Fold top half over filling to form a rectangle; seal edges with fork. Sprinkle, if desired, with ground cinnamon and sugar.

5. Bake 15 minutes or until crust is golden brown. Slice and serve warm with yogurt.

Skippy® Power Packs

8 servings Prep Time: *10 minutes* Cook Time: *9 minutes*

1 package (8 oz.) refrigerated crescent rolls
8 heaping tsp. Skippy® Peanut Butter
8 tsp. grape, strawberry or raspberry jelly

1. Preheat oven to 400°F. Spray baking sheet with nonstick cooking spray; set aside.

2. Separate dough into 8 triangles. Place 1 heaping teaspoon Skippy® Peanut Butter on each triangle, then top each with 1 teaspoon jelly.

3. Roll up triangles, starting at wide end. Fold sides under and pinch to seal.

4. On prepared baking sheet, arrange triangles. Bake for 9 minutes or until golden.

5. On wire rack, cool 2 minutes. Remove from baking sheet and cool completely. Serve warm or at room temperature.

Apple Pie with Peanut Butter Crumble

8 servings Prep Time: *10 minutes* Cook Time: *20 minutes*

1 can (21 oz.) apple pie filling

1 cup uncooked quick-cooking oats

1 cup all-purpose flour

1 cup firmly packed light brown sugar

⅓ cup Skippy® Creamy Peanut Butter

6 Tbsp. margarine

1. Preheat oven to 375°F. In 9-inch pie plate, evenly spread pie filling; set aside.
2. In medium bowl, combine oats, flour and brown sugar. With pastry blender or two knives, cut in Skippy® Creamy Peanut Butter and margarine until mixture is size of small peas. Sprinkle crumb mixture over pie filling.
3. Bake 20 minutes or until apples are heated through and topping is golden brown. Serve warm or cool.

Serving Suggestion Top, if desired, with vanilla ice cream.

Chocolate-Peanut Butter Strawberry Shortcake

12 servings Prep Time: *5 minutes* Cook Time: *40 minutes*

1 box (1 lb. 2.25 oz.) chocolate or yellow cake mix

3 cups frozen whipped topping, thawed

½ cup Skippy® Creamy Peanut Butter

2 cups sliced strawberries

1. Prepare, bake, and cool cake mix according to package directions for 13 x 9-inch baking pan.
2. In medium bowl, with wire whisk, beat whipped topping with Skippy® Creamy Peanut Butter. Spread evenly over cake, then top cake with strawberries.

Summer Sundae Ice Cream Pie

8 servings **Prep Time:** *15 minutes* **Chill Time:** *30 minutes*

½ gallon ice cream, slightly softened

9-inch chocolate crumb crust or graham cracker crust

½ to ¾ cup Skippy® Peanut Butter, melted

2 Tbsp. chocolate sprinkles

1. Scoop ice cream into prepared crust.

2. Drizzle with melted Skippy® Peanut Butter and sprinkles.

3. Cover and freeze until ready to serve. Let stand 5 minutes before slicing.

Serving Suggestion Garnish, if desired, with your favorite sundae toppings.

Peanutty Pie

8 servings Prep Time: *10 minutes* Cook Time: *55 minutes*

3 eggs

1 cup sugar

1 cup light or dark corn syrup

½ cup Skippy® Creamy Peanut Butter

2 Tbsp. margarine, melted

1 tsp. vanilla extract

1¼ cups unsalted peanuts

9-inch unbaked deep-dish pie crust*

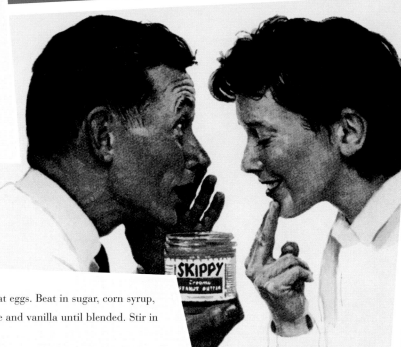

1. Preheat oven to 350°F.

2. In large bowl, with wire whisk or fork, beat eggs. Beat in sugar, corn syrup, Skippy® Creamy Peanut Butter, margarine and vanilla until blended. Stir in peanuts. Pour into piecrust.

3. Bake 55 minutes or until knife inserted halfway between center and edge comes out clean. On wire rack, let cool. Garnish, if desired, with whipped cream.

Tip *To use a frozen pie crust, do not thaw. Preheat oven and a cookie sheet. Pour filling into frozen crust. Bake on cookie sheet as above. (Insulated cookie sheet is not recommended.)

Peanut Butter Boston Cream Pie

12 servings **Prep Time:** *15 minutes* **Cook Time:** *30 minutes*
Chill Time: *45 minutes*

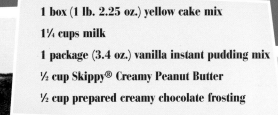

1 box (1 lb. 2.25 oz.) yellow cake mix

1¼ cups milk

1 package (3.4 oz.) vanilla instant pudding mix

½ cup Skippy® Creamy Peanut Butter

½ cup prepared creamy chocolate frosting

1. Prepare, bake, and cool cake mix according to package directions for 2 round cake pans.

2. In medium bowl, with electric mixer on medium speed, beat milk, pudding and Skippy® Creamy Peanut Butter 2 minutes or until blended.

3. Spread top of one cake layer with pudding mixture. Top with second cake layer, then spread top with frosting. Drizzle, if desired, with melted Peanut Butter.

8 servings Prep Time: *15 minutes* Chill Time: *1 hour*

2 cups milk

2 packages (3.9 oz. ea.) chocolate instant pudding mix

½ cup Skippy® Creamy Peanut Butter

1 container (8 oz.) frozen whipped topping, thawed

8-inch graham cracker crust or chocolate crumb crust

1. In large bowl, with electric mixer on low speed, beat milk, pudding and Skippy® Creamy Peanut Butter until blended, about 30 seconds. Beat on medium speed 2 minutes.

2. Fold in ½ of the whipped topping. Evenly spread filling into crust, then top with remaining whipped topping.

3. Refrigerate 1 hour or until set.

Chocolate Chip Peanut Butter Pound Cake

12 servings Prep Time: *15 minutes* Cook Time: *45 minutes*

1 box (1 lb. 2.25 oz.) yellow cake mix

1 cup milk

¾ cup Skippy® Creamy Peanut Butter

3 eggs

2 cups mini semi-sweet chocolate chips

1. Preheat oven to 350°F. Grease and lightly flour a 12-cup bundt pan or fluted tube pan; set aside.

2. In large bowl, with electric mixer at low speed, beat cake mix, milk, ½ cup Skippy® Creamy Peanut Butter and eggs until blended, about 1 minute. Beat at medium speed 2 minutes, scraping sides occasionally. Stir in 1 cup chocolate. Pour into prepared pan.

3. Bake 45 minutes or until toothpick inserted in center comes out clean. On wire rack, cool 10 minutes; remove from pan and cool completely.

4. Meanwhile, for icing, in medium microwave-safe bowl, microwave remaining 1 cup chocolate with ¼ cup Peanut Butter at HIGH 1 minute or until chocolate is melted; stir until smooth. Drizzle or spread over cooled cake and sprinkle, if desired, with chopped peanuts.

Holiday Entertaining

CHAPTER EIGHT

Peanut Butter Caramel Topping

about 1 cup topping Prep Time: 5 minutes Cook Time: 30 seconds

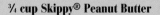

¾ **cup Skippy® Peanut Butter**

¼ **cup caramel topping**

¼ **cup milk**

1. In small microwave-safe bowl, combine all ingredients. Microwave at HIGH 30 seconds or until Skippy® Peanut Butter is melted; stir.

Serving Suggestion Serve, if desired, over fresh fruit or ice cream.

about 1 cup sauce **Prep Time: *5 minutes*** **Cook Time: *1 minute 30 seconds***

½ cup Skippy® Creamy Peanut Butter
¼ cup heavy or whipping cream
½ cup semi-sweet chocolate chips

1. In 1½-quart microwave-safe bowl, microwave Skippy® Creamy Peanut Butter and cream at HIGH 1½ minutes or until boiling. Add chocolate, stirring until melted. Store in tightly covered container in refrigerator.

Serving Suggestion Serve, if desired, over ice cream.

Skippy® Peanut Brittle

6 servings Prep Time: *5 minutes* Cook Time: *6 minutes*

1 cup sugar

½ cup light corn syrup

⅛ tsp. salt

1 cup peanuts, cashews or mixed nuts

½ cup Skippy® Creamy or Super Chunk® Peanut Butter

1½ tsp. baking soda

1. Spray baking sheet and metal spatula with nonstick cooking spray; set aside.

2. In 2-quart microwave-safe glass measuring cup or bowl, blend sugar, corn syrup, and salt.

3. Microwave at HIGH 5 minutes or until syrup is pale yellow. Stir in peanuts and Skippy® Peanut Butter.

4. Microwave 1 minute. Immediately stir in baking soda until foamy. Quickly pour onto prepared baking sheet and evenly spread with spatula.

5. Let cool, then break into pieces.

Tip Store in tightly covered container.

Peanut Butter Fudge

64 servings Prep Time: **10 minutes** Cook Time: **5 minutes**
Chill Time: **2 hours**

¼ cup margarine

¼ cup light corn syrup

1 jar (18 oz.) Skippy® Creamy Peanut Butter

1¼ cups confectioners sugar

1 tsp. vanilla extract

1. Spray 8-inch square baking pan with nonstick cooking spray; set aside.

2. In 2-quart saucepan, melt margarine with corn syrup over medium heat, stirring occasionally. Add Skippy® Creamy Peanut Butter and cook, stirring frequently, until smooth. Remove from heat.

3. With wooden spoon, stir in confectioners sugar and vanilla until smooth. Spread in prepared pan.

4. Refrigerate 2 hours or until firm. To serve, cut into 1-inch squares.

Nutshell Clusters

24 clusters Prep Time: **10 minutes** Chill Time: **30 minutes**

½ cup Skippy® Creamy Peanut Butter

1 cup butterscotch morsels or semi-sweet chocolate chips

1 cup whole salted peanuts

1. In medium microwave-safe bowl, microwave Skippy® Creamy Peanut Butter and butterscotch morsels at HIGH, stirring occasionally, 1½ minutes or until melted.

2. Stir in peanuts. Onto waxed-paper-lined baking sheet, drop mixture by teaspoonfuls.

3. Chill 30 minutes or until set.

Buckeyes

54 buckeyes Prep Time: *45 minutes* Cook Time: *5 minutes*
Chill Time: *1 hour*

½ cup Skippy® Peanut Butter

¾ cup margarine

2 cups confectioners sugar

1 package (6 oz.) semi-sweet chocolate chips (about 1 cup)

1. Line baking sheet with waxed paper or parchment paper; set aside.

2. In medium bowl, combine Skippy® Peanut Butter and ½ cup margarine until blended. Gradually stir in sugar.

3. On cutting board or flat surface, knead peanut butter mixture until smooth. Shape mixture into 54 (¾-inch) balls. Arrange balls on prepared baking sheet. Refrigerate for 30 minutes.

4. In 1-quart saucepan, melt chocolate and ¼ cup margarine over low heat, stirring occasionally.

5. Using two forks, dip balls into chocolate, covering ⅔ of ball and leaving one side exposed to resemble buckeyes. Return to baking sheet.

6. Refrigerate 1 hour or until firm. Store in tightly covered container in refrigerator.

Holiday Entertaining

24 servings Prep Time: *15 minutes* Cook Time: *25 minutes*

1 cup Skippy® Super Chunk® Peanut Butter

½ cup (1 stick) margarine, softened

¾ cup firmly packed light brown sugar

½ cup granulated sugar

1 tsp. vanilla extract

2 eggs

2 cups all-purpose flour

½ tsp. salt

1 package (12 oz.) semi-sweet chocolate chips

1 cup toffee bar bits

1. Preheat oven to 350°F. Grease 13 x 9-inch baking pan; set aside.

2. In large bowl, with electric mixer, beat Skippy® Super Chunk® Peanut Butter, margarine, brown sugar, granulated sugar and vanilla until thick and creamy, about 5 minutes. Beat in eggs, then flour blended with salt.

3. Stir in 1 cup chocolate chips. Evenly spread into prepared pan.

4. Bake 25 minutes or until lightly browned. Remove from oven to wire rack and immediately sprinkle with remaining chocolate chips. Let stand 5 minutes.

5. Evenly spread melted chocolate, then sprinkle with toffee bar bits; cool completely. To serve, cut into bars.

Sweet Ravioli Tartlets

15 servings Prep Time: *30 minutes* Cook Time: *9 minutes*

1 package (15 oz.) refrigerated pie crusts
1 scant cup Skippy® Peanut Butter
Your favorite jelly or jam
Confectioners sugar

1. Preheat oven to 425°F.

2. Place pie crusts on lightly floured surface. With 3-inch round cookie cutter, cut out rounds. Roll out unused dough and cut additional rounds.

3. Place 1 tablespoon Skippy® Peanut Butter in center of 15 rounds; top each with 1 teaspoon jelly.

4. Place remaining pie crust rounds on top and pinch or fold edges over to seal.

5. On ungreased baking sheet, arrange ravioli. Bake 9 minutes or until golden brown. On wire rack, cool 5 minutes. Serve warm, sprinkled with confectioners sugar.

Variation Use semi-sweet chocolate chips instead of jelly.

Peanut Butter Crunchers

24 servings Prep Time: *10 minutes* Cook Time: *1 minute*
Chill Time: *30 minutes*

1 cup butterscotch morsels or semi-sweet
chocolate chips
½ cup Skippy® Peanut Butter
2 cups chow mein noodles or crispy rice cereal

1. Line baking sheet with waxed paper; set aside.
2. In large microwave-safe bowl, microwave butterscotch morsels and Skippy® Peanut Butter at HIGH 30 seconds; stir.
3. Microwave an additional 30 seconds or until melted; stir until smooth. Stir in chow mein noodles.
4. On prepared baking sheet, drop mixture by rounded tablespoonfuls. Chill 30 minutes or until set.

Peanut Butter Lover's Cannoli Cups

6 servings Prep Time: *20 minutes*

1 cup ricotta cheese
½ cup Skippy® Peanut Butter
2 Tbsp. heavy or whipping cream
2 Tbsp. sugar
¼ cup mini semi-sweet chocolate chips
1 box (10 oz.) frozen puff pastry shells, prepared
according to package directions
½ cup hot fudge topping, heated

1. In large bowl, with wire whisk, blend ricotta, Skippy® Peanut Butter, cream and sugar. Stir in chocolate.
2. Generously fill each pastry shell with peanut butter mixture, then drizzle with hot fudge.

Peanut Butter Angel Trifle

10 servings Prep Time: 10 minutes Cook Time: 30 minutes

1 container (8 oz.) frozen whipped topping, thawed

½ cup Skippy® Peanut Butter

½ cup mini semi-sweet chocolate chips

1 angel food cake (about 13 oz.), cut into cubes

½ cup chopped pecans or walnuts, toasted if desired

1. In large bowl, with wire whisk, thoroughly blend whipped topping and Skippy® Peanut Butter. Stir in chocolate.
2. In serving bowl, arrange ½ of the cake cubes, then evenly top with ½ of the peanut butter mixture and ½ of the nuts. Repeat layers ending with nuts.
3. Chill 30 minutes or until ready to serve.

Peanut Butter & Chocolate Crescents

24 servings Prep Time: *30 minutes* Cook Time: *9 minutes*

1 package (15 oz.) refrigerated pie crusts

Skippy® Creamy or Super Chunk® Peanut Butter (about 1 cup)

Semi-sweet chocolate chips

Confectioners sugar

1. Preheat oven to 425°F.

2. Place pie crusts on lightly floured surface. With 3-inch round cookie cutter, cut out rounds. Roll out unused dough and cut additional rounds.

3. Place ½ tablespoon Skippy® Creamy Peanut Butter in center of each round; top each with a few chocolate chips. Fold dough over to form a crescent, pinching edges to seal. (Crescents may open a little during baking.)

4. On ungreased baking sheet, arrange crescents. Bake 9 minutes or until golden brown. Serve warm, sprinkled with confectioners sugar.

Peanut Butter Tiramisu

8 servings **Prep Time:** *20 minutes* **Chill Time:** *30 minutes*

2 small bananas, thinly sliced

2 Tbsp. light rum

1 container (8 oz.) frozen whipped topping, thawed

½ cup Skippy® Peanut Butter

1 package (3 oz.) prepared ladyfingers (about 24)

3 ounces strong brewed coffee or espresso

Cocoa powder

1. In medium bowl, gently toss bananas with rum; set aside.

2. In large bowl, with wire whisk, blend whipped topping with Skippy® Peanut Butter.

3. On serving platter, arrange ladyfingers, top sides down, into four rows of three to form a rectangle. Brush each ladyfinger generously with coffee.

4. Evenly top ladyfingers with ½ of the peanut butter mixture, then top with bananas. Brush remaining coffee on bottoms of remaining ladyfingers and arrange, top sides up, on bananas.

5. Evenly spread remaining peanut butter mixture on top and sides, then sprinkle with cocoa powder.

6. Chill 30 minutes or until ready to serve. Sprinkle, if desired, with additional cocoa powder.

Holiday Entertaining

Peanut Butter 'N Chocolate Dipped Strawberries

about 20 servings Prep Time: *5 minutes* Cook Time: *2 minutes*

1 cup Skippy® Creamy Peanut Butter

1 cup semi-sweet chocolate chips

1 qt. dipping strawberries

1. In medium microwave-safe bowl, microwave ½ cup Skippy® Creamy Peanut and chocolate at HIGH, stirring occasionally, 1½ minutes or until mixture is melted and smooth.
2. Dip strawberries in peanut butter mixture, then let stand on waxed-paper-lined baking sheets until chocolate is set, about 30 minutes.
3. In small microwave-safe bowl, microwave remaining ½ cup Peanut Butter at HIGH 30 seconds or until melted. Stir, then drizzle over dipped strawberries.

Variation Try dipping pretzels, marshmallows, shortbread cookies, or bananas.

Baked Peanut Butter Turnovers

4 servings Prep Time: *5 minutes* Cook Time: *15 minutes*

1 can (10 oz.) refrigerated pizza crust
½ cup Skippy® Creamy Peanut Butter
½ cup applesauce
¼ tsp. sugar
¼ tsp. ground cinnamon

1. Preheat oven to 400°F.

2. Unroll crust. With rolling pin or your hands, press into an 8 x 12-inch rectangle, then cut into 4 rectangles.

3. On greased baking sheet, arrange rectangles. Evenly spread with Skippy® Creamy Peanut Butter, then top with applesauce, leaving ½-inch border around edges. Fold top half over filling to form a triangle; seal edges with fork, then sprinkle with sugar and cinnamon.

4. Bake 15 minutes or until crust is golden brown. Serve warm.

Peanut Butter Pumpkin Pie

8 servings **Prep Time: *5 minutes* Cook Time: *65 minutes***

3 eggs

1 can (16 oz.) pumpkin

½ cup firmly packed light brown sugar

½ cup granulated sugar

½ cup Skippy® Creamy Peanut Butter

2 tsp. pumpkin pie spice*

½ tsp. salt

½ pint light cream or half & half

9-inch unbaked deep-dish pie crust

1. Preheat oven to 350°F.

2. In large bowl, with wire whisk, beat eggs. Beat in pumpkin, sugars, Skippy® Creamy Peanut Butter, pumpkin pie spice and salt.

3. Gradually add light cream, beating until blended; pour into pie crust.

4. Bake for 65 minutes or until knife inserted in center comes out clean. On wire rack, let cool.

*Substitution: Use ½ teaspoon EACH ground cinnamon, nutmeg, ginger, and allspice.

Serving Suggestion Garnish, if desired, with whipped cream.

Holiday Entertaining

Island Ambrosia

5 servings Prep Time: *10 minutes*

1 container (8 oz.) frozen whipped topping, thawed

½ cup Skippy® Peanut Butter

1 can (11 oz.) mandarin oranges, drained

1 can (8 oz.) pineapple tidbits or crushed pineapple in natural juice, drained

4 large bananas, sliced

1 cup flaked coconut, toasted (optional)

Ground cinnamon

1. In large bowl, with wire whisk, thoroughly blend whipped topping and Skippy® Peanut Butter.

2. Stir in oranges, pineapple and bananas.

3. Top with coconut and sprinkle with cinnamon. Chill, if desired, until ready to serve.

Fluffy Skippy® Dessert Dip

2 cups dip **Prep Time: *5 minutes***

¼ cup Skippy® Creamy Peanut Butter
1 package (8 oz.) cream cheese, softened
1 jar (7 oz.) marshmallow cream

1. In medium bowl, blend Skippy® Creamy Peanut Butter with cream cheese, then blend in marshmallow cream.

Serving Suggestion Serve, if desired, with fresh fruit, butter cookies or crackers, or use as a frosting for cake or cupcakes.

141

Acknowledgments

Editor: Lecia Monsen

Book Designer: Matt Shay

Photography: Aristo Studios

Contributing Writer: Christine Allen-Yazzie

Home Economist: Krista Winston

Norman Rockwell images reproduced by permission of the Norman Rockwell Family Agency, Inc.

Metric Conversion Chart

inches to millimeters and centimeters							*weights* and measures
inches	*mm*	*cm*	*inches*	*cm*	*inches*	*cm*	3 teaspoons = 1 tablespoon
⅛	3	0.3	9	22.9	30	76.2	4 tablespoons = ¼ cup
¼	6	0.6	10	25.4	31	78.7	5⅓ tablespoons = ⅓ cup
½	13	1.3	12	30.5	33	83.8	8 tablespoons = ½ cup
⅝	16	1.6	13	33.0	34	86.4	10⅔ tablespoons = ⅔ cup
¾	19	1.9	14	35.6	35	88.9	12 tablespoons = ¾ cup
⅞	22	2.2	15	38.1	36	91.4	16 tablespoons = 1 cup
1	25	2.5	16	40.6	37	94.0	1 tablespoon = ½ fluid ounce
1¼	32	3.2	17	43.2	38	96.5	1 cup = 8 fluid ounces
1½	38	3.8	18	45.7	39	99.1	1 cup = ½ pint
1¾	44	4.4	19	48.3	40	101.6	2 cups = 1 pint
2	51	5.1	20	50.8	41	104.1	4 cups = 1 quart
2½	64	6.4	21	53.3	42	106.7	2 pints = 1 quart
3	76	7.6	22	55.9	43	109.2	4 quarts = 1 gallon
3½	89	8.9	23	58.4	44	111.8	1 tablespoon = 14.79 milliliters
4	102	10.2	24	61.0	45	114.3	1 cup = 236.6 milliliters
4½	114	11.4	25	63.5	46	116.8	1.06 quarts = 1 liter
5	127	12.7	26	66.0	47	119.4	1 pound = 453.59 grams
6	152	15.2	27	68.6	48	121.9	1 ounce = 28.35 grams
7	178	17.8	28	71.1	49	124.5	
8	203	20.3	29	73.7	50	127.0	

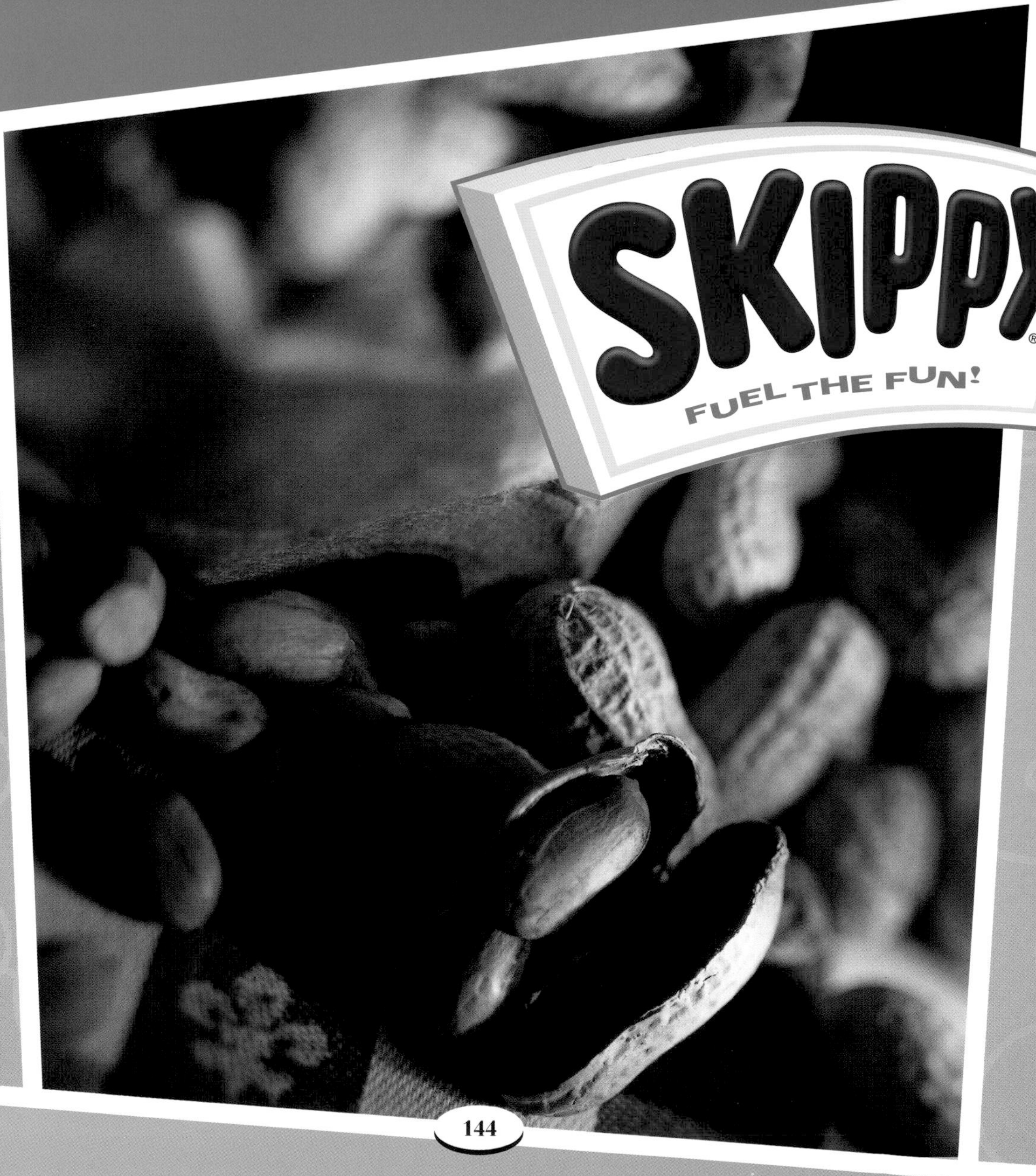
SKIPPY®
FUEL THE FUN!